Patagonia Revisited

Patagonia Revisited

BRUCE CHATWIN AND
PAUL THEROUX

Illustrated by
KYFFIN WILLIAMS

HOUGHTON MIFFLIN COMPANY

BOSTON

1986

First American edition 1986

Text copyright © 1986 by Bruce Chatwin and
Cape Cod Scriveners Company
Illustrations copyright © 1986 by Kyffin Williams

Library of Congress Catalog Card Number 85–42941

Designed by Humphrey Stone

Set in Palatino
Printed and bound in Great Britain

About the Artist

Kyffin Williams was born in 1918 in Llangefni, Anglesey, and studied at the Slade School of Art 1941–44. He was elected Associate of the Royal Academy in 1970, and Royal Academician in 1974. In 1968 he was awarded the Winston Churchill Fellowship to record the Welsh in Patagonia. His autobiography, *Across the Straits*, was published in 1973.

BRUCE CHATWIN: Since its discovery by Magellan in 1520, Patagonia was known as a country of black fogs and whirlwinds at the end of the habited world. The word 'Patagonia', like Mandalay or Timbuctoo, lodged itself in the Western imagination as a metaphor for The Ultimate, the point beyond which one could not go. Indeed, in the opening chapter of *Moby Dick*, Melville uses 'Patagonian' as an adjective for the outlandish, the monstrous and fatally attractive:

> Then the wild and distant seas where he rolled his island bulk; the undeliverable, nameless perils of the whale: these, with all the attending marvels of a thousand Patagonian sights and sounds, helped sway me to my wish.

Paul and I went to Patagonia for very different reasons. But if we are travellers at all, we are literary travellers. A literary reference or connection is likely to excite us as much as a rare animal or plant; and so we touch on some of the instances in which Patagonia has affected the literary imagination.

We are also both fascinated by exiles. If the rest of the world blew up tomorrow, you would still find in Patagonia an astonishing cross-section of the world's nationalities, all of whom have drifted towards these 'final capes of exile' for no other apparent reason than the fact that they were there.

On any one day in Patagonia, the traveller could expect to encounter a Welshman, an English gentleman-farmer, a Haight-Ashbury Flower Child, a Montenegran nationalist, an Afrikaaner, a Persian missionary for the Bahai religion, or the Archdeacon of Buenos Aires on his round of Anglican baptisms.

Or there would be characters like Bautista Dias Low, a horse-tamer and Anarchist, whom I met near Puerto Natales in Southern Chile; and who, with his own hands, had hacked himself a cattle ranch from the rain forest. He surprised me with some intricate knowledge about the voyage of the *Beagle*: not that he had read books about it, or could even read, but because his great-grandfather, Captain William Low, had been Darwin and FitzRoy's pilot through the *canales*. It was generous of him to attribute his courage and absolute bloody-mindedness to his *sangre britannica*.

The earliest travellers to Patagonia definitely mistook it for the Land of the Devil. For one, the mainland was inhabited by a race of giants – the Tehuelche Indians, who turned out, on closer acquaintance, to be less gigantic and less fierce than their reputation – and may indeed have given Swift his model for the coarse but amiable inhabitants of Brobdingnag.

Patagonia was also a land of strange beasts and birds. 'Pen-gwyn' is thought to be a Welsh expression for 'flightless bird'; the Elizabethan sailors had a superstition that jackass penguins were the souls of their drowned comrades; and, in the seventeenth century, Sir John Narborough, visiting Puerto Deseado, described them as 'standing upright like little children in white aprons in company together'. There was the condor, which somehow got confused with Zeus's eagle and Sinbad the Sailor's roc; and it was off the coast of Tierra del Fuego that Captain Shelvocke, an eighteenth-century English privateer, saw an albatross:

> The heavens were perpetually hid from us by gloomy dismal clouds . . . one would think it impossible that any living thing could subsist in so rigid a climate; and, indeed . . . we had not had the sight of one fish of any kind . . . nor one sea-bird, except a disconsolate black *albitross* . . . hovering about us as if he had lost himself, till *Hatley* (my second Captain) observing, in one of his melancholy fits, that this bird was always hovering near us, imagined, from his colour, that it might be some ill omen . . . [and] after some fruitless attempts, at length, shot the *Albitross*, not doubting (perhaps) that we should have a fair wind after it. . . .

This text, of course, read first by Wordsworth and passed on to Coleridge, became:

'In mist or cloud, on mast or shroud,
It perched for vespers nine;
Whiles all the night, through fog-smoke white,
Glimmered the white Moon-shine.'

'God save thee, ancient Mariner!
From the fiends, that plague thee thus! –
Why look'st thou so?' – 'With my cross-bow
I shot the Albatross.'*

Nor did the later nineteenth century do anything to dispel the idea that Patagonia was a Land of Marvels. The moment scientists, such as Darwin, scratched the soil, they found it to be a boneyard of prehistoric mammals, some of which were thought to be alive. They also found petrified forests, fizzling lakes, and glaciers of blue ice sliding through forests of southern beech.

*Since we gave the lecture, another fatal shooting took place in these waters – the sinking of the Argentine cruiser *Belgrano* by a British submarine on 2 May 1982. A day or so later, a journalist commented that this action would prove to be 'Mrs Thatcher's albatross' without, perhaps, being aware of the literary reverberations. The mate Hatley shot his bird just after the ship had rounded the easternmost cape of Tierra del Fuego; the *Belgrano* was outside the war zone, heading back towards Tierra del Fuego when the torpedoes hit.

PAUL THEROUX: When I think of going anywhere, I think of going south. I associate the word 'south' with freedom, and at a very young age I bought Sir Ernest Shackleton's book *South* for the title alone. My first job was in the southern part of Nyasaland, and it wasn't a bad choice: there I could think straight, and began for the first time in my life to write.

I had nothing to do, so I decided to go to Patagonia. It was an easy choice. I knew it was the emptiest part of America and one of the least known – consequently a forcing-house of legends, half-truths and misinformation. And it was reachable by land. There is no greater pleasure than waking in the morning in Boston and knowing that you are to travel 15,000 miles and not have to board an aeroplane. (I was wrong about that, but I didn't know it at the time.) Patagonia seemed like a precinct of my own country, the people there called themselves Americans. Looking at the map it seemed that by moving south I could pass through Mexico, sprint across Central America and entering the great funnel of South America drop slowly down the Andes and roll naturally into Patagonia, where I would come to rest. It was snowing in Boston when I left: Patagonia promised a different climate, a change of mood, and complete freedom to wander.

That is the best mood to have when starting out. I was willing, I was game; it is only later, in travel, that one understands that the greatest distance inspires the greatest illusions, and that solitary travel is both a pleasure and a penalty.

Patagonia has not been widely photographed. I had no mental image of it, only the fanciful blur of legend, the giants on the shore, the ostrich on the plain, and a sense of displaced people, like my own ancestors who had fled from Europe. When I tried to call up an image of Patagonia, nothing came and I was as helpless as if I had tried to describe the landscape of a distant planet or paint the smell of an onion. The unknown landscape is justification enough for going to it.

My other reason was plainer. In 1901, my great-grandfather left Italy for Argentina. He was fifty-two and had had a fairly miserable life, farming in a small village called Agazzano, near Piacenza. Argentina was America, an *estancia*, a better life; he had four children. He knew what he was in for – other Italians had gone and sent back reports that it was a good place for Italians to settle. Indeed, there were so many Italians there that W. H. Hudson was convinced that the place was spoiled for ever – one of his reasons for not ever going back to Argentina was that the Italians had interfered with the bird life.

Anyway, this man Francesco Calesa packed his bags for Argentina. He was not unusual. Thousands were doing the same. But when he got to the boat he was told that there had been an outbreak of yellow fever in Buenos Aires, no one could go to Argentina, and the ship was re-routed to New York. With some misgivings, Calesa, with his wife and four children, went to New York. He hated New York at once, and from the moment of his arrival plotted his escape. But his wife wouldn't go, and when Calesa finally fled America, the marriage was fractured, Calesa was alone and ageing and no longer confident enough to start again in Argentina.

So Patagonia was the promise of an unknown land-scape, the experience of freedom, the most southerly part of my own country, the perfect destination; but it was also a way of completing the trip my great-grandfather had wanted to make.

And when, after the long trip, I arrived in Patagonia I felt I was nowhere. But the most surprising thing of all was that I was still in the world – I had been travelling south for months. The landscape had a gaunt expression, but I could not deny that it had readable features and that I existed in it. This was a discovery – the look of it. I thought: *Nowhere is a place*.

Down there the Patagonian valley deepened to grey rock, wearing its aeons' stripes and split by floods. Ahead, there was a succession of hills, whittled and fissured by the wind, which now sang in the bushes. The bushes shook with this song. They stiffened again and were silent. The sky was clear blue. A puff of cloud, white as a quince flower, carried a small shadow from town, or from the South Pole. I saw it approach. It rippled across the bushes and passed over me, a brief chill, and then it went rucking east. There were no voices here. There was this, what I saw; and though beyond it were mountains and glaciers and albatrosses and Indians, there was nothing here to speak of, nothing to delay me further. Only the Patagonian paradox: tiny blossoms in vast space; to be here, it helped to be a miniaturist, or else interested in enormous empty spaces. There was no intermediate zone of study. Either the enormity of the desert or the sight of a tiny flower. In Patagonia you had to choose between the tiny or the vast.

BRUCE CHATWIN: For me, Patagonia was a Land of Marvels from the precocious age of three. In my grandmother's cabinet of curiosities there was a piece of animal's skin with coarse reddish hair, stuck to a card with a rusty pin.

'What's that?' I asked, and was told: 'A piece of brontosaurus' – or at least, that is what I thought I was told.

The story, as I knew it, was that my grandmother's cousin, Charley Milward the Sailor, had found a brontosaurus perfectly preserved in a glacier in Tierra del Fuego. He had it salted, packed in barrels and sent to the Natural History Museum in South Kensington. Unfortunately, though, it went rotten on its voyage through the tropics, and that was why you saw a brontosaurus skeleton in the Museum, but no skin. He had, however, sent a little piece to my grandmother, by post.

The story, of course, was untrue; and it was a terrible blow, at the age of nine or so, to learn that brontosauruses had no hair, but scaly, armoured hide. The beast of my childhood dreams turned out, in fact, to be the mylodon, or giant sloth* – an animal that died out in Patagonia about 10,000 years ago, but whose skin, bones and excrement were found, conserved by dryness and salt, in a cave at Last Hope Sound, in the Chilean province of Magallanes.

My cousin Charley was an eccentric, somewhat peppery captain of the New Zealand Shipping Company, whose first command, the *Mataura*, got wrecked on Desolation Island, at the entrance to the Strait of Magellan, in 1898. While salvaging the wreck, he succumbed to the lure of the Far South and settled in the gloomy port of Punta Arenas, where he bought a share in an iron foundry. In 1904 he became British Consul, and when he came to build a house, he reconstructed, out of homesickness, his father's parsonage in Birmingham: the neighbours used to say, 'I suppose he thinks he'll go to Heaven quicker in a place like that.' It was in this house, in 1915, that Sir Ernest Shackleton stayed during those terrible

*Bones of the mylodon were found by Darwin at Punta Alta. See Alan Moorehead, *Darwin and the Beagle*, pp. 82–7.

days waiting for the Chilean Navy to send its tug, the *Yelcho*, to fetch his men off Elephant Island.

Twelve years before that, however, Charley had helped a half-mad German gold-panner called Albert Konrad to dynamite the cave for mylodon skin and bones which, by that time, had become a saleable commodity to the natural history museums of Europe. Some zoologists, including Sir Arthur Smith Woodward, had thought the beast was still alive, and the *Daily Express* financed an expedition to find it. They failed, of course, but the episode left its mark on literature, in that it seems to have been an ingredient of Conan Doyle's *The Lost World*.

Never have I wanted anything as I wanted that piece of skin. But when my grandmother died, it got thrown away, and I vowed that, one day, I would go and find a replacement. This spurious quest ended, one stormy afternoon in 1976, when I sat at the back of the cave, after finding a few strands of mylodon hair and a lump of mylodon dung, which looked a bit like last week's horse (so much so that my cleaning lady took exception to it and, the other day, chucked it out). At the moment of discovery I heard voices chanting, 'Ave Maria!' – and thought I'd definitely gone mad. The singers were the nuns from a convent in Punta Arenas on their Saturday afternoon bus tour. I had already seen them, the week before, on another visit, at the penguin colony on Cabo Virgines.

My piece of dung wasn't exactly the Golden Fleece, but

it did give me the idea for the form of a travel book, for the oldest kind of traveller's tale is one in which the narrator leaves home and goes to a far country in search of a legendary beast.

PAUL THEROUX: Within a few years of Darwin's visit (1832) to Patagonia, an American family migrated to Argentina and settled in the Rio de la Plata region, about ten miles from Buenos Aires. They were among the first Americans there, and they were Yankees to the core: the man was born in the Massachusetts seaport of Marblehead, his wife – descended from Pilgrim Fathers – was from Maine. They farmed with little success, but remained in Argentina for the rest of their lives. These were the parents of W. H. Hudson, who was born in Quilmes in 1841.

He had a strange pedigree for someone who considered himself English. For thirty-two years he lived in Argentina; he spent one year in Patagonia, around the Rio Negro. In 1868 his father died and he left South America and went to England, where he remained, living largely in penury, his wife running one unsuccessful boarding house after another. He died on the top floor of the last boarding house, in North Kensington – in the small room where he had worked. It must have been hell, because he was six foot three.

He appears to have been the serenest man imaginable: he never forgot Patagonia and never stopped writing about it. What he sought in England was its Patagonian-like places – in Cornwall and on Salisbury Plain, the flat, wind-swept and unpeopled districts. He described himself as 'a naturalist in the old, original sense of the word, who is mainly concerned with the "life and conversation of animals"'.

Jorge Luis Borges once said: 'You will find nothing there. There is nothing in Patagonia. That's why Hudson liked it. You will notice there are no people in his books.'

This is partly true, and in *Idle Days in Patagonia* Hudson *(What)* suggests a reason: 'In spite of what we have been taught, it is sometimes borne in on us that man is a little lower than the brutes.' Hudson's books are peculiar. Some are entirely about birds. One novel, *A Crystal Age*, preaches against the sexual impulse. In this he advances the view that Industrialism, with its uncreative tasks, accentuates the sexual urge; the weakness of man is that he is oversexed. He believed the best recourse was for society to model itself on the beehive, with one woman in a community as the child-bearing queen bee. The central thought, he wrote to Edward Garnett, was that there would be no peace on earth until that sexual 'fury has burnt itself out'. He married at the age of thirty-five; his wife was fifty. They had no children.

The message of *Idle Days in Patagonia*, which was written in a London boarding house in 1893, is in Hudson's own capital letters: TRY PATAGONIA. Patagonia is the cure for mankind's ills. It is also the occasion for a man to see how mistaken Darwin, Melville and Leigh Hunt were in their various literary flights. It is full of rebuttal, it refutes fanciful notions and its closest kin in literature is Thoreau's *Walden*.

In Hudson's view, the experience of Patagonia is a journey to a higher plane of existence, to a kind of harmony with nature which is the absence of thought; Hudson called this 'animism', the intense love for the visible world.

In the last chapter of Darwin's *Voyage of the Beagle* there is a paragraph which goes as follows:

. . . In calling up images of the past, I find that the plains of Patagonia frequently cross before my eyes; yet these plains are pronounced by all wretched and useless. They can be described only by negative characters; without habitations, without water, without trees, without mountains, they support only a few dwarf plants. Why, then, and the case is not peculiar to myself, have these arid wastes taken so firm a hold of my memory? Why have not the still more level, the greener and more fertile Pampas, which are serviceable to mankind, produced an equal impression? I can scarcely analyse these feelings; but it must be partly owing to the free scope given to the imagination. The plains of Patagonia are boundless, for they are scarcely passable, and hence unknown; they bear the stamp of having thus lasted, as they are now, for ages, and there appears no limit to their duration through future time. If, as the ancients supposed, the flat earth was surrounded by an impassable breadth of water, or by deserts heated to an intolerable excess, who would not look at these last boundaries to man's knowledge with deep but ill-defined sensations?

Hudson understands Darwin's bafflement, but he is not sympathetic to it. Darwin's mistake was that he was looking for something in Patagonia, as in other times people looked for the Andean valley of Trapalanda with its White Indians, or the fabled city of Manoa sought for by Alonzo Pizarro; it is better, Hudson says, to look for nothing at all. Feel it, he says, and be moved by it.

Judging from my own case [Hudson says] I believe that we have here the secret of the persistence of the Patagonian images, and their frequent recurrence in the minds of many who have visited that grey, monotonous, and, in one sense, eminently uninteresting region. It is not the effect of the unknown, it is not imagination; it is that nature in these desolate scenes . . . moves us more deeply than in others.

Later, he becomes specific:

One day while *listening* to the silence, it occurred to my mind to wonder what the effect would be if I were to shout aloud. This seemed at the time a horrible suggestion of fancy, a 'lawless and uncertain thought' which almost made me shudder, and I was anxious to dismiss it quickly from my mind. But during those solitary days it was a rare thing for any thought to cross my mind; animal forms did not cross my vision or bird-voices assail my hearing more rarely. In that novel state of mind I was in, thought had become impossible . . . I had become incapable of reflection: my mind had suddenly transformed itself from a thinking machine into a machine for some other unknown purpose. To think was like setting in motion a noisy engine in my brain; and there was something there which bade me be still, and I was forced to obey. My state was one of *suspense* and *watchfulness*: yet I had no expectation of meeting with an adventure, and felt as free from apprehension as I feel now when sitting in a room in London . . . I was powerless to wonder at or speculate about it; the state seemed familiar rather than strange, and although accompanied by a strong feeling of elation, I did not know it – did not know that something had come between me and my intellect – until I lost it and returned to my former self – to thinking, and the old insipid existence.

Why should this be so in Patagonia, and not in a

tropical forest? Well, Hudson says, the tropical forest is
full of variety – noise, bird song, colour, animal life: the
senses are engaged, but,

> . . . in Patagonia the monotony of the plains, or
> expanse of low hills, the universal unrelieved greyness
> of everything, and the absence of animal forms and
> objects new to the eye, leave the mind open and free to
> receive an impression of nature as a whole. . . . It has a
> look of antiquity, of desolation, of eternal peace, of a
> desert that has been a desert from of old and will
> continue a desert for ever; and we know that its only
> human inhabitants are a few wandering savages – who
> live by hunting as their progenitors have done for
> thousands of years.

Emptiness, desolation, the suspension of intellect:
Hudson recommended these things when he was miser-
able in London and remembered the land of lost content.
What is Hudson's Patagonia? It is the opposite of a
London boarding house.

He had found in Patagonia an American Eden, a
peaceable kingdom, where you could see a cow lying
down and twenty-six wild pigs using her for a pillow. To
be in Patagonia was to surrender to nature and, paradox-
ically, passion was abolished – none of that fury, only the
contentment of the beehive. He speaks with horror of
'books written indoors', of Darwin calling some animals

ugly, of the pointlessness of newspapers and the affairs of the world.

How should one die? The perfect death is Patagonian:

The man who finishes his course by a fall from his horse, or is swept away and drowned when fording a swollen stream, has, in most cases, spent a happier life than he who dies of apoplexy in a counting-house or dining-room; or who, finding that end which seemed so infinitely beautiful to Leigh Hunt (which to me seems so unutterably hateful), drops his white face on the open book before him.

But this, the unutterably hateful way, was how Hudson died.

BRUCE CHATWIN: Hudson was wrong in his prediction that Patagonia would remain a desert. The South, at least, turned out to be some of the finest sheep country in the world; and, within thirty years, sheep companies, many of them British, had taken over the territory. The province of Santa Cruz became a country of big houses and shooting parties. My cousin Charley managed to get hold of some of the best land for himself, at Valle Huemeules, within sight of the Cordillera – although he was soon to lose it through the machinations of a 'land-shark who has kindly sworn that my house and all my animals are his'.

While visiting the glacier of Lago Argentino, I called in at the Estancia La Anita, which belongs to the Menendez-Behety family, the sheep-farming moguls of the South. It was here in 1921 that an army of Anarchist revolutionaries, led by a Spanish ex-circus acrobat called Antonio Soto, held hostage about thirty British and other farm managers. When, finally, they surrendered to the Argentine Army, about a hundred and twenty men – nearly all Chileans – were shot into graves they dug themselves, their leaders having nipped away and escaped over the border.

Not all the colonization of Patagonia was like this. Among the immigrants were simple Scottish crofters who had come by way of the Falklands – but the firstcomers, as everyone knows, were the Welsh.

They were refugees from cramped coal-mining valleys and unworkable farms who, just before Hudson's time, went to the Chubut River with the intention of founding a New Wales: indeed, there is a case for supposing that modern Welsh nationalism began with the Patagonia colony.

The movement was led by the Revd Michael Jones of Bala, whose agents combed the earth for a stretch of territory unoccupied and uncontaminated by the Union Jack. He had hoped for a mass exodus, but when the time

came to leave, there were only a hundred and fifty-three takers – all of whom landed at Puerto Madryn in 1865 off the chartered brig *Mimosa*.

The Welsh are still there. The Eisteddfod is still sung in St David's Hall in Trelew, and around the village of Gaiman there are farms that take you back to the simple agricultural world of Parson Kilvert. It is a little strange for an Englishman to have to speak Spanish to a Mr Jones or a Mr Griffiths. On one farm I met a Mr Williams, whose first cousin, Dr Bryn Williams, came back to Wales, and is now the Archdruid.

By the end of the 1880s the Welsh had outgrown their settlement in the valley; and some of them migrated up river, and carved themselves sheep farms in the foothills of the Cordillera. The village they founded is called Trevelin, the 'Place of the Mill'. The country around it is exactly like parts of Wyoming or Utah; and it's hardly surprising that, when law and order settled in, like a blight, over the American West, some of the more enterprising spirits came down to start a New West in the Absolute South.

One of these characters was a 'defrocked' Texas sheriff called Martin Sheffield, who had a Patagonian career as gold-panner, sharpshooter and minor crook. In 1922 he announced his discovery of a living dinosaur, a plesiosaurus, in a lake near Epuyen – and made world headlines. (The lake is two and a half feet deep.) Various right-wing newspapers in Buenos Aires found it most flattering to think that Argentina had a Loch Ness Monster of its own – though as a left-wing daily commented: 'This millenarian, pyramidal, apocalyptic animal makes a noise like a madonna and usually appears in the opaline stupors of drunken gringos.'

At the bar in Epuyen, while following up the plesiosaurus story, I talked to some gauchos (this being Patagonia, they were Arab gauchos) whose leader told me that a pair of North American bandits had been living about twenty kilometres along the road at Cholila. I went there next morning and found a perfect specimen of a Western log cabin surrounded by poplars and a corral. The owner said it must have been a beautiful place once and, pointing to the flowered paper coming in shreds off the walls, said: 'Si, señor, there was a film made about those two gentlemen.'

A few months later I was sitting in the State Historical Society of Utah reading this letter, written in the cabin and dated 10 August 1902:

My dear friend,

I suppose you have thought long before that I had forgotten you (or was dead) but, my dear friend, I am still alive, and when I think of my old friends you are always the first to come to mind. It will probably surprise you to hear from me away down in this country but U.S. was too small for me the last two years I was there. I was restless. I wanted to see more of the world. I had seen all of the U.S. that I thought was good . . . another of my uncles died and left $30,000 to our little family of 3 so I took my $10,000 and started to see a little more of the world. I visited the best cities and the best parts of South A. till I got here. And this part of the country looked so good that I located, and I think for good, for I like the place better every day. I have 300 cattle, 1,500 sheep, and 28 good saddle horses, 2 men to do my work, also a good 4 room house, warehouse, stable, chicken house and some chickens. The only thing lacking is a cook, for I am living in single cussidness [*sic*] and sometimes I feel very lonely for I am alone all day, and my neighbours don't amount to anything, besides the only language spoken in this country is Spanish, and I don't speak it well enough to converse on the latest scandals so dear to the hearts of all nations. . . .

The writer was an ex-Mormon called Robert Leroy Parker, better known as Butch Cassidy, at that time the most wanted outlaw in the United States, with a string of perfectly executed bank and train robberies behind him. The recipient of the letter, back in Utah, was a Mrs Davies, mother-in-law of Cassidy's greatest friend, Elza Lay. The 'little family of 3' was a *ménage à trois* consisting of Cassidy, Harry Longabaugh – the 'Sundance Kid' – and the Kid's wife, a beautiful schoolteacher from Denver called Etta Place – who may or may not have been the granddaughter of the 5th Earl of Essex. The 'dead uncle' who gave them the $30,000 was the Wild Bunch Gang's robbery on the First National Bank of Winnemucca, Nevada, on 10 September 1900.

This was their last hold-up in the United States. Already the pace had got too hot for them when the Union Pacific Railroad put mounted rangers in their box cars. The purpose of the robbery was to get enough money to set sail for South America. After it was over, the disbanded Wild Bunch Gang rode to Fort Worth; had their farewell photograph taken, and sent a copy to the bank manager in Winnemucca, in whose office it still hangs.

The 'little family of 3' then went to New York, where the Kid bought Etta a gold watch at Tiffany's; and they both had their photograph taken again. They also went to the Metropolitan Opera where the Kid, whose real name was Leinbach, is said to have become a devoted Wagnerian. They sailed to Buenos Aires, won a concession of land at Cholila, and settled there. Three years later, possibly to finance a trip to Europe (one outlaw historian claims they went to the Bayreuth Festival), they staged a bank robbery in Rio Gallegos, the Argentine port near the Straits of Magellan. On returning from Europe, they settled again in Cholila, but soon afterwards, with the help of the New York photograph, they were traced there by the Pinkerton Agency. They sold the cabin and left in a hurry, for Bolivia, where they are supposed to have died in a shootout with the Army – at least, this is the version you see in the movie.

But I must warn anyone who is tempted to take up outlaw history that it is a most dementing subject, in that your characters can have up to ten aliases and die in ten different places. The Pinkerton Agency has three different deaths for Butch Cassidy on its files, none of them in Bolivia. For myself, I would like to think that Cassidy and his gang returned from Bolivia in 1909; that, in a fracas with the Argentine Frontier Police, the Kid was killed in 1910; and that Cassidy himself went back to the United States and died in his bed. In 1925 he is supposed to have revisited his old horse-dealer at Sheep Creek Canyon,

Utah; and to have stayed again in the cabin where, between train robberies, he would hole up and read the works of Lord Macaulay. He is also supposed to have eaten blueberry pie with his old father in the family house at Circleville: at least that is what his sister told me, Lula Parker Betenson, still very much alive at the age of ninety-four.

PAUL THEROUX: The first sighting of a giant was reported by Antonio Pigafetta who kept a journal during the three years (1519–22) when he sailed with Magellan on the first voyage round the world. It was round about September 1521 near San Julian:

> . . . One day, without anyone expecting it, we saw a giant, who was on the shore of the sea, quite naked, and was dancing and leaping, and singing, and whilst singing he put the sand and dust on his head. Our captain sent one of his men towards him, whom he charged to sing and leap like the other to reassure him, and show him friendship. This he did, and immediately the sailor led this giant to a little island where the captain was waiting for him; and when he was before us he began to be astonished, and to be afraid, and he raised one finger on high, thinking that we

came from heaven. He was so tall that the tallest of us only came up to his waist. . . .

The giant's face was painted red and yellow, with two hearts painted on his cheeks, and his nearly hairless head was painted white. He wore well-sewn clothes of skins and thick fur boots on his feet. Shown his image in a mirror, he was terrified and enraged.

. . . The captain named this kind of people Pataghom [on account of their large feet]* who have no houses, but have huts made of the skins of the animals with which they clothe themselves, and go hither and thither with these huts of theirs, as the gypsies do; they live on raw meat, and eat a certain sweet root, which they call Capac. These two giants that we had in the ship ate a large basketful of biscuit, and rats without skinning them, and they drank half a bucket of water at each time.

Magellan decided to kidnap two giants as a present for Charles V and his Queen Empress. The two giants had been tricked into being manacled, but when they saw they were caught they puffed and blew and they foamed 'like bulls, crying out very loud "Setebos", that is to say, the great devil, that he should help them'. There was a

*An editorial interpolation in the 1874 edition.

great fuss, and a fight, but in time both giants were baptized. Though the idea was to bring the Big-Feet back to Spain, the giants died – the one baptized Paulo in the Pacific – and only Pigafetta's written account was to return.

Shakespeare read the account. The evidence is in *The Tempest*. Compare

. . . he raised one finger on high, thinking that we came from heaven

with

Caliban: Hast thou not dropped from heaven?

Stephano: Out o' the moon, I do assure thee: I was the man in the moon, when time was.

Compare

. . . crying out . . . 'Setebos', . . . the great devil

with

Caliban: I must obey: his art is of such power
It would control my dam's god, Setebos,
And make a vassal of him.

The giants were described by other early explorers: de Weert, Spelbergen and Shelvocke, and they adopted Magellan's term, *Patagones*, 'big feet'. Byron's grand-father met the Big-Feet and in a curious picture he is

shown watching a giant Patagonian woman rather anx-
iously – he comes up to her midriff. How he happened to
be in Patagonia is a long story, of shipwreck and
starvation and heroic survival, which Peter Shankland
tells in *Byron of the Wager*. Shankland writes:

> Thomas Cavendish had measured the imprint of one of
> their feet and found it to be eighteen inches long. Byron
> on tip-toes could just reach the top of the head of one of
> the Patagonians.
>   Their middle stature seemed to be about eight feet;
> 'their extreme, nine and upwards', one of his officers
> wrote. The giants, with time, seemed to be getting
> more gigantic; their feet, in successive reports, even
> bigger.

'Patagons' are mentioned by Thomas Falkner in his *A
Description of Patagonia* (1774). Falkner arrived in Argentina quite by chance in 1731. He was unwell, but was
looked after by some Irish Jesuits and in time became a
convert to the Catholic faith, and travelled throughout
Patagonia as a missionary. Falkner said that the Tehuel-
ches are known in Europe 'by the name of Patagons' and
though he attests to their great size, he describes the
human bones he has found as even more enormous:

> On the banks of the River Carcarania, or Tercero,
> about three or four leagues before it enters into the

Parana, are found great numbers of bones, of an extraordinary bigness, which seem human. There are some greater and some less, as if they were of persons of different ages. I have seen thigh-bones, ribs, breast-bones, and pieces of skulls. I have also seen teeth, and particularly some grinders which were three inches in diameter at the base. These bones (as I have been informed) are likewise found on the banks of the Rivers Parana and Paraguay. . . . The Indian historian, Garcilasso de la Vega Inga, makes mention of these bones in Peru, and tells us that the Indians have a tradition, that giants formerly inhabited those countries, and were destroyed by God for the crime of sodomy.

This book was studied by Darwin and was in the library of the *Beagle* (Darwin refers to the author as 'Falconer'). Darwin, in consequence, was on the lookout for the giants. In Cape Gregory, he writes,

We had an interview . . . with the famous so-called gigantic Patagonians, who gave us a cordial reception. Their height appears greater than it really is, from their large guanaco mantles, their long flowing hair, and general figure: on an average their height is about six feet, with some men taller and only a few shorter; and the women are also tall; altogether they are certainly the tallest race which we anywhere saw.

Their faces were painted; they spoke a little English and Spanish because they had had contact with sealers and whalers. He found them half-civilized and 'proportionally demoralized'.

Fifty years later, Lady Florence Dixie set sail for Patagonia ('Land of the Giants') 'because it was an outlandish place and so far away'. With her were Lord Queensberry, Lord James Douglas, her husband and brothers.

> We only took one servant with us, knowing that English servants inevitably prove a nuisance and hindrance in expeditions of the kind, when a great deal of 'roughing it' has to be gone through, as they have an unpleasant knack of falling ill at inopportune moments.

After some months of travel they found themselves (at Punta Arenas) in the presence of a real Patagonian Indian. They thought him a 'singularly unprepossessing object, and, for the sake of his race, we hoped an unfavourable specimen of it'. He was dirty, but Lady Florence was further disappointed by his size and the size of his fellow tribesmen:

> I was not struck so much by their height as by their extraordinary development of chest and muscle. As regards their stature, I do not think the average height of the men exceeded six feet, and as my husband

stands six feet two inches I had a favourable opportunity for forming an accurate estimate. One or two there were, certainly, who towered far above him, but these were exceptions.

In one respect, Lady Florence was satisfied: on the Indians' feet were boots, large, and appropriately Patagonian.

In *The Tempest*, Caliban seems to stand for 'the betrayed native'. In Pigafetta and in Falkner, the Indians are large and handsome and numerous. Darwin reports them as not so numerous, not very big, and rather miserable and abject. They have been visited by Europe, and diminished by it. Lady Florence Dixie sees them as 'fast approaching extinction' and smaller than her husband and, she says, 'numbering no more than 800 souls'. Fifty years later, the Patagonian giants – or rather one small Patagonian Indian – were gone.

BRUCE CHATWIN: And yet Patagonia cannot, and never could have meant Big-Foot. 'Pata' is indeed a 'foot' or 'hoof' in Spanish but the suffix '–gon' is meaningless. Even Drake's chaplain, Francis Fletcher, knew there was something wrong and tried to turn the Patagonians into 'Pentagours' – meaning 'five cubits high', which would

bring them to seven and a half feet. And then my attention was drawn to a late medieval romance called *Primaleon of Greece,* in which a strange beast called Patagon appears.

The book was written by an unknown author and published in Spain in 1512, that is, seven years before Magellan sailed. It was translated by Shakespeare's friend Anthony Mundy in 1596, fifteen years before *The Tempest.* I believe that both Magellan and Shakespeare read it.

Primaleon of Greece is one of those interminable sagas which, in the sixteenth century, were considered extremely exciting. It runs to about 800 packed pages, and was the kind of book an explorer might take on a long journey as we might take away Proust. The most famous example of the genre was the *Book of Amadis*.

In the first book of *Primaleon*, the hero dashes around Europe, rescues damsels in distress, fights giants, helps the Emperor of Constantinople against the Turks, makes friends with Prince Edward of England, and does all the respectable things a knight should do. Then, at the end of Book II, he sails to a faraway island, where the King's son, a boy called Prince Palantine, tells him of a people who live in the hinterland – absolute savages who eat raw flesh and wear the skins of beasts:

> But this is nothing, in regard of one of them, which most usually is seene, and whom we call Patagon, said to be engendred by a Beast in the woods, being the strangest misshapen and counterfeite creature in the world. He hath good understanding, is amorous of women, and keepeth company with one of whom (it is said) he was engendred. . . .

In other words, Patagon is a latter-day equivalent of Grendel.

> He hath the face of a Dogge, great eares, which hang down upon his shoulders, his teeth sharpe and big, standing out of his mouth very much: his feete are like a Hart's, and he runneth wondrous lightly. Such as have seene him tell mervallous matters of him,

because he chaseth ordinarily among the mountaines with two Lyons in a chaine like a lease, and a bow in his hand. . . .

The moment the Knight hears of Patagon, he decides to go out hunting; and, after a tremendous struggle, fells him with two sound strokes of his sword:

Now through the grievous paine he [Patagon] felt by his wounds, as also his losse of blood, which dyed the grasse round about him, he was no longer able to stand on his legs, but falling on the earth, roared so dread-fully, as it would have terrified the very stoutest heart. . . .

With a right and a left, the Knight then gets rid of the two lions; trusses Patagon up with their leashes, and ships him aboard as a present for Queen Gridonia of Polonia, because, secretly, he is in love with her daughter, the Princess Zephira. On the journey the Patagon behaves quite dreadfully, but finally they reach port, where the Queen is persuaded to go on board ship. She takes one look at the monster and says: 'This can be nothing else but a divel . . . hee gets no cherishing at my hands.'

The Princess Zephira, however, is a far more spirited girl than her mother. She takes an immediate fancy to the Beast and advances

. . . boldly to Patagon, bidding him go along with her, stroking his head and using him very kindely: which made him forget his former stubbornesse, and fall at her feete, for he greatly delighted to gaze faire ladies in the face, so taking his chaine in her hand, he followed after her as gently, as if he had beene a Spaniell. . . .

We should perhaps explain here that the 'Giant' Tehuelche Indians were reported, as early as the sixteenth century, to have worn dog-headed 'vizzards' or masks – which is why Magellan would have said, 'Ha! Patagon!' when he saw one of these creatures dancing on the shore at St Julian. It will also explain why, in *The Tempest*, the comic Stephano says of Caliban, 'I shall laugh myself to death at this puppy-headed monster.'

I think we have here a situation in which a bad novel inspired a great explorer to do something shoddy, which, in turn, inspired the greatest playwright to one of his greatest creations.

PAUL THEROUX: The Fuegian Indians confirmed Darwin's ideas about the origins of our species and his suspicions that some men had evolved further than others. It was the Indian as a fisherman and a canoe-maker that interested him and other travellers to Patagonia. These are the key texts. ·

[Pigafetta] . . . In this place they have boats, which are made of a tree, all in one piece, which they call 'canoo'. These are not made with iron instruments, for they have not got any, but with stones, like pebbles, and with these they plane and dig out these boats. Into these thirty or forty men enter, and their oars are made like iron shovels; and those who row these oars are black people, quite naked and shaven, and look like enemies of hell. . . .

[Francis Fletcher] This cannowe, or boate, was made of the barke of divers trees, having a prowe and a sterne standing up, and semicirclewise yeelding inward, of one form and fashion, the body whereof was a most dainty mould, bearing in it most comely proportion and excellent workmanship, in so much as to our Generall and us, it seemed never to have beene done without the cunning and expert judgement of art; and that not for the use of so rude and barbarous a people, but for the pleasure of some great and noble personage, yea, of some Prince. It had no other closing up or caulking in the seames, but the stitching with thongs made of seal skins, or other such beast, and yet so close that it received very little or no water at all.

[Falkner] These Indians live near the sea, on both sides

of the straits. . . . They are sometimes attacked by the
Huilliches, and the other Tehuelhets, who carry them
away for slaves, as they have nothing to lose but their
liberty and their lives. They live chiefly on fish: which
they catch, either by diving, or striking them with their
darts. They are very nimble of foot, and catch guana-
coes and ostriches with their bowls [bolas]. Their
stature is much the same as that of the other
Tehuelhets, rarely exceeding seven feet, and often-
times not six feet. They are an innocent, harmless
people.

[Darwin] December 17th, 1832. . . . When we came
within hail, one of the four natives who were present
advanced to receive us, and began to shout most
vehemently, wishing to direct us where to land. When
we were on shore the party looked rather alarmed, but
continued talking and making gestures with great
rapidity. It was without exception the most curious and
interesting spectacle I ever beheld: I could not have
believed how wide was the difference between savage
and civilised man; it is greater than between a wild and
domesticated animal, inasmuch as in man there is a
greater power of improvement. . . .

December 25th. . . . While going one day on shore
near Wollaston Island, we pulled alongside a canoe
with six Fuegians. These were the most abject and
miserable creatures I anywhere beheld . . . [they] were

quite naked, and even one full-grown woman was absolutely so. It was raining heavily, and the fresh water, together with the spray, trickled down her body. In another harbour not far distant, a woman, who was suckling a recently-born child, came one day alongside the vessel, and remained there out of mere curiosity, whilst the sleet fell and thawed on her naked bosom, and on the skin of her naked baby! These poor wretches were stunted in their growth, their hideous faces bedaubed with white paint, their skins filthy and greasy, their hair entangled, their voices discordant, and their gestures violent. Viewing such men, one can hardly make oneself believe that they are fellow-creatures, and inhabitants of the same world. . . .

Their country is a broken mass of wild rocks, lofty hills, and useless forests; and these are viewed through mists and endless storms. The habitable land is reduced to the stones on the beach; in search of food they are compelled unceasingly to wander from spot to spot, and so steep is the coast that they can only move about in their wretched canoes. They cannot know the feeling of having a home, and still less that of domestic affection; for the husband is to the wife a brutal master to a laborious slave. . . . Their skill in some respects may be compared to the instinct of animals; for it is not improved by experience: the canoe, their most ingenious work, poor as it is, has remained the same, as we know from Drake, for the last two hundred and fifty years. . . .

BRUCE CHATWIN: One of the books that Darwin took aboard the *Beagle* was Captain James Weddell's *Voyage towards the South Pole* (in the brig *Jane* and the cutter *Beaufoy*). Weddell sailed further south than anyone had yet ventured, and on 8 February 1822, at latitude 74° 15' he saw whales, 'birds of the blue petrel kind', and leagues of open sea. He wrote on his chart: 'Sea of George IV – Navigable', and left the impression that the sea became warmer as one neared the Pole.

Returning northwards to the Cape Horn Archipelago, at Hermit Island he ran in with canoeloads of Fuegians who threatened to overrun the ship. He managed to persuade them to sit still while he read a chapter of the Bible – to which they listened with solemn faces, one man believing that the book itself talked.

Weddell then jotted down some words of their language and concluded that it was Hebrew, though how it had travelled to Cape Horn was, he admitted, 'a question of interest to philologists'.

Now it happened that, while Darwin was writing his *Journal* during the voyage of the *Beagle*, a copy of Captain Weddell's book lay on the desk of the editor of the *Southern Literary Messenger* in Richmond, Virginia – Edgar Allen Poe.

Poe himself was a solitary wanderer, obsessed by voyages of annihilation and rebirth; and he used Weddell's *Voyage towards the South Pole* to help him write his novel of a crazed, self-destructive journey. In *The Narrative of Arthur Gordon Pym*, the narrator lands on a warm Antarctic island called Tsalal where everything is black, including the bestial savages who swarm aboard the ship called *Jane*. Their language, too, is a variety of Hebrew – in other words, the Tsalalians are Fuegians transformed into fiction, with a smattering of Poe's own anti-Negro prejudices thrown in.

Pym is one of the nastiest, most brilliant and, in its effect on the imagination, influential books of the nineteenth century. It inspired Dostoevsky to write one of his rare literary essays; and because Baudelaire was its translator into French, it inspired a whole series of 'voyage' poems – from Baudelaire's own incomparable 'Le Voyage' ('Mais les vrais voyageurs sont ceux-là qui partent seulement pour partir . . . ')to Rimbaud's prose poem 'Being Beauteous'.

But the Fuegians themselves, who helped to set all this off, were a rather gentle people, who lived according to the rhythm of the seasons, and were contented with their lot. Towards the end of the last century, the Revd Thomas Bridges settled on the Beagle Channel as a missionary; and before his Indians died out, from epidemics, he managed to compile a dictionary of their language. This dictionary is now their monument. It would perhaps have surprised Darwin to learn that a young man of the Yaghan tribe had a vocabulary of around 30,000 words, perhaps even more than Shakespeare ever wrote. If anyone has time to spare, I do recommend them to take a look at Bridges's original manuscript in the British Museum: for the images that surface from its pages of crabbed handwriting are often of unimaginable beauty.

PAUL THEROUX: Nor is it fair to judge the Indians from that most memorable passage in Captain Joshua Slocum's *Sailing Alone around the World* (1900):

> . . . the natives, Patagonian and Fuegian . . . were as squalid as contact with unscrupulous traders could make them. A large percentage of the business there [in Punta Arenas] was traffic in 'fire-water'. If there was a law against selling the poisonous stuff to the natives, it was not enforced. Fine specimens of the Patagonian race, looking smart in the morning when they came into town, had repented before night of ever having seen a white man, so beastly drunk were they, to say nothing about the peltry of which they had been robbed. . . . Just previous to my arrival the governor, himself of a jovial turn of mind, had sent a party of young bloods to foray a Fuegian settlement and wipe out what they could of it on account of the recent massacre of a schooner's crew somewhere else. . . . The port captain, a Chilean naval officer, advised me to ship hands to fight Indians in the strait farther west, and spoke of my stopping until a gunboat should be going through, which would give me a tow. I said no more about the matter, but simply loaded my guns. At this point in my dilemma Captain Pedro Samblich, a good Austrian of large experience, coming along, gave me a bag of carpet-tacks, worth more than all the fighting men and dogs of Tierra del Fuego. I protested

that I had no use for carpet-tacks on board. Samblich smiled at my want of experience, and maintained stoutly that I would have use for them. 'You must use them with discretion,' he said; 'that is to say, don't step on them yourself.' With this remote hint about the use of the tacks I got on all right, and saw the way to maintain clear decks at night without the care of watching. . . .

Soon he is in the middle of the Strait, passing Thieves' Bay, 'suggestively named':

. . . As drowsiness came on I sprinkled the deck with tacks, and then I turned in, bearing in mind the advice of my old friend Samblich that I was not to step on them myself. I saw to it that not a few of them stood 'business end' up; for when the *Spray* passed Thieves' Bay two canoes had put out and followed in her wake, and there was no disguising the fact any longer that I was alone.

Now, it is well-known that one cannot step on a tack without saying something about it. A pretty good Christian will whistle when he steps on the 'commercial-end' of a carpet tack; a savage will howl and claw the air, and that was just what happened that night about twelve o'clock, while I was asleep in the cabin, where the savages thought they 'had me', sloop and all, but changed their minds when they stepped on deck, for then they thought that I or someone else had them. I had no need of a dog; they howled like a pack of hounds. I had hardly use for a gun. They jumped pell-mell, some into their canoes and some into the sea, to cool off, I suppose, and there was a deal of free language over it as they went. I fired several guns when I came on deck, to let the rascals know that I was home, and then I turned in again, feeling sure I should not be disturbed any more by people who left in so great a hurry.

The Fuegians, being cruel, are naturally cowards. . . .

And then there were none. . . . The extinction of the Yaghan, a rough parallel of what happened to all the Fuegian tribes, is recorded as follows:

Date		Yaghan
1834	The year the *Beagle* left Tierra del Fuego	3,000
	Then came the sealers and the whalers	
1880	Missionaries counted 7,000 to 8,000 among all the tribes. There would be	1,200
1888	Barclays's estimate	800
1889	Argentine Government distributed clothes to the shivering, half-starved Yaghan, and counted	400
1908	Barclay counted again	170
1924	Lothrop's figures	50

Lothrop wrote in 1925:

Later in the same year [1925] an epidemic of measles ravaged Tierra del Fuego. What happened to the Yaghan I do not know, but Mr William Bridges wrote me that more than twenty adult Ona and an unknown number of children had died. With the exception of a few mixed bloods the Indians of Tierra del Fuego are probably extinct.

All that is left of them is a monument in the little plaza of Ushuaia, '*al Indio*'.

BRUCE CHATWIN: Tierra del Fuego is, of course, 'The Land of Fire'; and the most usual explanation of its origin is that Magellan saw the camp fires of the Indians and called it 'Fireland'. Someone else has suggested that there were active volcanoes at the time; but this is not, geologically, correct. Another version says that Magellan saw the smoke of the camp fires only; called it Tierra del Humo; but that the Emperor Charles V, seeing that name on a map, said there was no smoke without fire, and changed it.

The evidence for the first explanation comes from Maximilian Transylvanicus, the man who interviewed the survivors on their return to Spain:

The month of November was upon them, the night was rather more than five hours long, and they had never seen any human beings on the shore. But one night a great number of fires were seen, mostly on their left hand, from which they guessed that they had been seen by the natives of the region. But Magellan, seeing that the country was rocky and also stark with eternal cold, thought it useless to waste many days in examining it.

Magellan was wise to move on; for the weather in the Strait is usually infernal. In fact, he was so exceptionally lucky that when he sailed out into what is usually one of the most violent seas in the world, he chanced on a flat calm, and called it the Pacific.

There is, however, another dimension to the Fireland problem. Cape Horn was rounded for the first time in 1619 by two Dutchmen, Schouten and Le Maire, who named the headland, not after its shape, or the shape of South America, but from their home port, Hoorn, in Holland. Before that, Tierra del Fuego was thought to be the tip of the Unknown Antarctic Continent, the Antichthon or Anti-Earth, whose existence was originally postulated by Pythagoras. The Antichthon was an upside-down country, absolutely not meant for human beings, where snow fell upwards, trees grew downwards, the sun shone black, and its inhabitants were the sixteen-fingered Antipodeans who danced themselves into ecstasy. 'We cannot go to them,' it was said. 'They cannot come to us.' It was, in other words, some kind of Hell. Small wonder, then, that Magellan refused to land.

For, from the moment America had been discovered, from the moment that the discoveries of Columbus and Vespucci were recorded by the cartographers of Europe, it was obvious that a Strait of Water had to separate this Dreadful Place from the rest of creation. One map-maker, Martin of Bohemia, accordingly took the obvious step of drawing in the Strait, which Magellan proceeded to discover.

The issue was further complicated by certain medieval notions about the Other Side of the Globe. Dante, for example, believed with the Greeks that the entire Southern Hemisphere was uninhabited, uninhabitable and thus out of bounds for man. One of the most arresting passages in the *Inferno* relates the southern voyage of Ulysses in search of the Mountain of Purgatory, which lay at the heart of the Antichthon, and from which no man returned. Dante takes as his starting point the lines of the *Odyssey* where the blind prophet, Tiresias, predicts that the hero will not be content to sit at home with Penelope in Ithaca, but that death will come to him from out of the sea. In Canto 26, Dante and Virgil find Ulysses burning in the Eighth Ring of Hell for having attempted to reach the forbidden mountain, not as a dead soul, but as a living man thirsting for knowledge.

Here, in one of the greatest of all passages that describe the explorer's passion to get to the back of beyond, is Ulysses' own account of how he persuaded his men to follow him out of the Mediterranean, and through the Pillars of Hercules:

'O brothers,' I said, 'who through a hundred thousand dangers have reached the west, to this so brief vigil of our senses that remains to us, choose not to deny experience, following the sun, of the world that has no people. Consider your origin: you were not made to live as brutes, but to pursue virtue and knowledge.'

With this little speech I made my companions so keen for the voyage that then I could hardly have held them back. And turning our stern to the morning, we made of our oars wings for the mad flight, always gaining on the left. The night now saw the other pole and all its stars, and ours so low that it did not rise from the ocean floor. Five times the light beneath the moon had been rekindled and as many quenched, since we had entered on the passage of the deep, when there appeared to us a mountain dark in the distance, and to me it seemed the highest I had ever seen. We rejoiced, but soon our joy was turned to grief, for from the new land a whirlwind rose and struck the forepart of the ship. Three times it whirled her round with all the waters, and the fourth time it lifted the stern aloft and plunged the prow below, as pleased Another, till the sea closed over us.

And this, of course, is the passage that gave Tennyson the idea for his own 'Ulysses':

It little profits that an idle king,
By this still hearth, among these barren crags,
Matched with an agèd wife, I mete and dole,
Unequal laws unto a savage race,
That hoard, and sleep, and feed, and know not me.
I cannot rest from travel: I will drink
Life to the lees . . .

PAUL THEROUX: Canto 26 also gave Poe the end to *The Narrative of Arthur Gordon Pym*; for when the hero finally escapes from the island of Tsalal in a canoe, he plunges on southwards into a vortex of destruction:

> March 22. The darkness had materially increased, relieved only by the glare of the water thrown back from the white curtain before us. Many gigantic and pallidly white birds flew continuously now from beyond the veil, and their scream was the eternal *Tekeli-li!* as they retreated from our vision. Hereupon Nu-Nu stirred in the bottom of the boat; but upon touching him, we found his spirit departed. And now we rushed into the embraces of the cataract, where a chasm threw itself open to receive us. But there arose in our pathway a shrouded human figure, very far larger in its proportions than any dweller among men. And the hue of the skin of the figure was of the perfect whiteness of the snow.

And here, in yet another variant, is the sinking of the *Pequod* from *Moby Dick*:

> For an instant, the tranced boat's crew stood still; then turned. 'The ship? Great God, where is the ship?' Soon they through dim, bewildering mediums saw her sidelong fading phantom, as in the gaseous Fata Morgana; only the uppermost masts out of water;

while fixed by infatuation, or fidelity, or fate, to their once lofty perches, the pagan harpooners still maintained their sinking look-outs on the sea. And now, concentric circles seized the lone boat itself, and all its crew, and each floating oar, and every lance-pole, and spinning, animate and inanimate, all round and round in one vortex, carried the smallest chip of the *Pequod* out of sight.

BRUCE CHATWIN: To return to Dante: in the second book of the *Divine Comedy*, the 'Purgatorio', Dante and Virgil emerge from Hell; travel across a solitary plain; see from afar 'the trembling of the sea', and finally come to a desert shore 'that never saw any man navigate its waters who afterwards had experience of return'. Standing at the water's edge, they meet the souls of the dead who await the Boatman to ferry them across the water to the Mountain of Purgatory: the summit they can see in the distance. Dante, too, waits his turn; but, unlike Ulysses, he has been fortunate enough to pluck the Golden Bough – which is his passport to return to the land of the living.

Now when the truth of Magellan's discoveries began to filter through Europe, the poets, at least, saw him as a new Ulysses. And even Magellan himself, as he careered on his south-westerly course down the coast of Patagonia, must have been reminded of the archetypal mariner's 'mad track' to the bottom of the globe. The mutinies he had to suppress testify to the terror of his men; and when they peered across the Strait at the north shore of Fireland, they could perhaps be forgiven for mistaking the Fuegian camp fires for dead souls burning in Hell.

Certainly, the poets of Renaissance Europe were soon busy weaving mythologies out of Magellan, of Ulysses, of Straits, of Ferrymen, Death and Resurrection. One was the Andalucian Don Luis de Góngora, who, in his *First Solitude*, describes Magellan's Strait as 'the elusive hinge of silver':

> Hinge that unites, one ocean, the two seas,
> Whether the carpet of the morning star
> It kisses, or the rocks of Hercules.

But no one has ever described the 'south-west passage' to the next life more wonderfully than John Donne on his deathbed:

> Since I am comming to that Holy roome,
>   Where, with thy Quire of Saints for evermore,
> I shall be made thy Musique; As I come
>   I tune the Instrument here at the dore,
>   And what I must doe then, thinke here before.

Whilst my Physitians by their love are growne
   Cosmographers, and I their Mapp, who lie
Flat on this bed, that by them may be showne
   That this is my South-west discoverie
   Per fretum febris, by these streights to die,

I joy, that in these straits, I see my West;
   For, though theire currants yeeld returne to none,
What shall my West hurt me? As West and East
   In all flatt Maps (and I am one) are one,
   So death doth touch the Resurrection.

Is the Pacifique Sea my home? Or are
   The Easterne riches? Is *Jerusalem?*
Anyan, and *Magellan*, and *Gibraltare*,
   All streights, and none but streights, are wayes to
      them,
   Whether where *Japhet* dwelt, or *Cham*, or *Sem*.

We thinke that *Paradise* and *Calvarie*,
   Christs Crosse, and *Adams* tree, stood in one place;
Looke Lord, and finde both *Adams* met in me;
   As the first *Adams* sweat surrounds my face,
   May the last *Adams* blood my soule embrace.

So, in his purple wrapp'd receive mee Lord,
   By these his thornes give me his other Crowne;
And as to others soules I preach'd thy word,
   Be this my Text, my Sermon to mine owne,
   Therfore that he may raise the Lord throws down.

Imagine my delight then to find that the legend of the Boatman survives quite independently among the Indians in this part of the world. My last days in the South were spent on the soft green island of Chiloe, which traditionally sends its young men as migrant workers to the sheep ranches of Patagonia. The island is all but divided by two lakes, Huillinco and Cucao, which flow out into the Pacific, and along which the souls of the dead are thought to be ferried before crossing the sea to the other world.

I found the road to Cucao as bad as it had been in Darwin's day: so, like him a hundred and forty years before, I decided to take the ferry. Had he, however, known the legend of the Ferryman, I doubt he'd have risked this note in his diary:

The periagua was a strange rough boat, but the crew were even stranger. I doubt if six uglier little men ever got into a boat together.

Cucao, when I got there, reminded me of those reconstructions of Norse settlements you sometimes see in Scandinavian museums. In the largest house I was offered a bed and, that evening, by the fireside, I met an old Indian story-teller called Don Antonio. He told of Millalobo, a kind of merman who'd made off with one of the neighbour's daughters and taken her to live in a palace at the bottom of the lagoon. He told of sea-monsters, the Basilisk, the Thrauco, the Sirens and the Pincoya, a red-haired sea-nymph who encouraged the shellfish to multiply.

In the last of the light, he pointed to a black rock at the end of the bay and said it was the Boatman's landing-stage.

'Once,' he said, 'I knew a man who laughed at the story of the Boatman. We warned him; but he went out there, and stood on the rock, and shouted, "Boatman! Boatman!" – and the Boatman came.'

Sources

The Poems of Samuel Taylor Coleridge, edited by Ernest Hartley Coleridge, London, 1931.

Dante Alighieri, *The Divine Comedy*, translated by Charles S. Singleton, London, 1971–5.

Darwin, Charles, *Journal of Researches into the Natural History and Geology of the Countries Visited during the Voyage round the World of H.M.S. Beagle* . . . London, 1902.

Dixie, Lady Florence, *Across Patagonia*, London, 1880.

The Poems of John Donne, edited by Sir Herbert Grierson, Oxford, 1933.

The World Encompassed by Sir Francis Drake . . . Carefully Collected out of the Notes of Master Francis Fletcher, London, 1628.

Falkner, Thomas, *A Description of Patagonia*, Hereford, 1774.

Góngora y Argote, Luis de, *The Solitudes*, translated by Edward Meryon Wilson, Cambridge, 1965.

Hudson, W. H., *Idle Days in Patagonia*, London, 1893.

Lothrop, Samuel Kirkland, *The Indians of Tierra del Fuego*, New York, 1928.

The First Voyage round the World, by Magellan, translated from the accounts of Pigafetta, and other contemporary writers, edited by Lord Stanley of Alderley, Hakluyt Society, vol. LII, London, 1874.

Melville, Herman, *Moby Dick*, London, 1946.

Poe, Edgar Allan, *The Narrative of Arthur Gordon Pym*, New York, 1960.

The Famous and Renowned Historie of Primaleon of Greece, translated by A[nthony] M[unday], London, 1619.

Shankland, Peter, *Captain Byron of the Wager*, London, 1975.

Shelvocke, George, *A Voyage round the World*, London, 1726.

Slocum (Joshua), *Sailing Alone around the World*, London, 1900.

The Poems of Tennyson, edited by Christopher Ricks, London, 1969.